Lovable Bears

BY JENNY McWHINNEY

The bear quilt holds special memories for me. We were about to go on a family holiday, driving from Adelaide to Melbourne, across to Tasmania on the ferry, and then drive around the island for two weeks. My husband, Ron, had the car packed to bursting and our two daughters, Jess and Sarah-Kate, were so excited they were running back and forth saying, "Hurry up, Mum! We're going, we're going!"

I was crouched behind the sofa where I kept my box of wools and spare blanketing. I knew we were going to spend a lot of time in the car so I needed something to do. I was madly cutting 12 squares of blanketing to put in my wool box with my needles, sketch pad and pencil. This box was going to spend the next two weeks on my knee while Ron was driving.

I had no great plans about what I wanted to do - I just felt I wanted to embroider a little bear.

The drive to Melbourne was amazing. It rained non-stop. The window wipers were working overtime. It poured. So as I sketched the little bear I thought it only right that he should be wearing a little yellow raincoat and one of my favourite hats, a sou'wester, and gumboots.

I really enjoyed stitching the little fellow and as we boarded the Spirit of Tasmania, I looked out to the ocean in front of us and

decided I should do another little bear this time in a sailor suit.

When we docked in Devonport, Jess seemed a little off-colour and I suspected an ear infection, so as soon as we could, we went to the local doctor. The nurse-come-receptionist was so sweet, I thought I should dedicate a bear to her. So now we had Nurse Bear.

We drove to Launceston and as we walked through this lovely town we passed the University and I could just imagine a bear on graduation day. I imagined all the knowledge contained in all the libraries of all the universities of the world. Hence the birth of Bookworm Bear.

We then drove to beautiful Cradle Mountain and then to Opossum Bay. As we passed the quaint churches on the way, I imagined how important these meeting places must have been to the women all those years ago living on isolated farms. It must have been a life-line to meet with other women to talk about 'women's things' such as sewing, cooking and companionship. So I sketched a little Lady Bear in her Sunday bonnet.

We walked along the beach at Opossum Bay and the wind blew cold. I thought how brave you would have to be to go for a dip in the chilly Pacific Ocean. That's how Bathing Bear developed.

The visit to Port Arthur brought about a mass of inspiration -

almost too much to bear! After my visit I couldn't sketch fast enough. I imagined the soldiers marching up and down in their uniforms guarding the convicts, and the insignificant crimes these people were supposed to have committed. I remembered the English Bobbies in their uniforms, even though they were of a different era.

As we strolled around this fantastic place I could see the difference between the convict quarters and the homes of the officers and dignitaries. So I sketched a bear in a top hat and tails.

As we drove back to Devonport, nearing the end of our wonderful trip, I asked the girls "What other bears could I draw?" Jess called out, "A Ballerina Bear!" and Sarah shouted, "No! A clown bear!"

So I did both.

Jenny

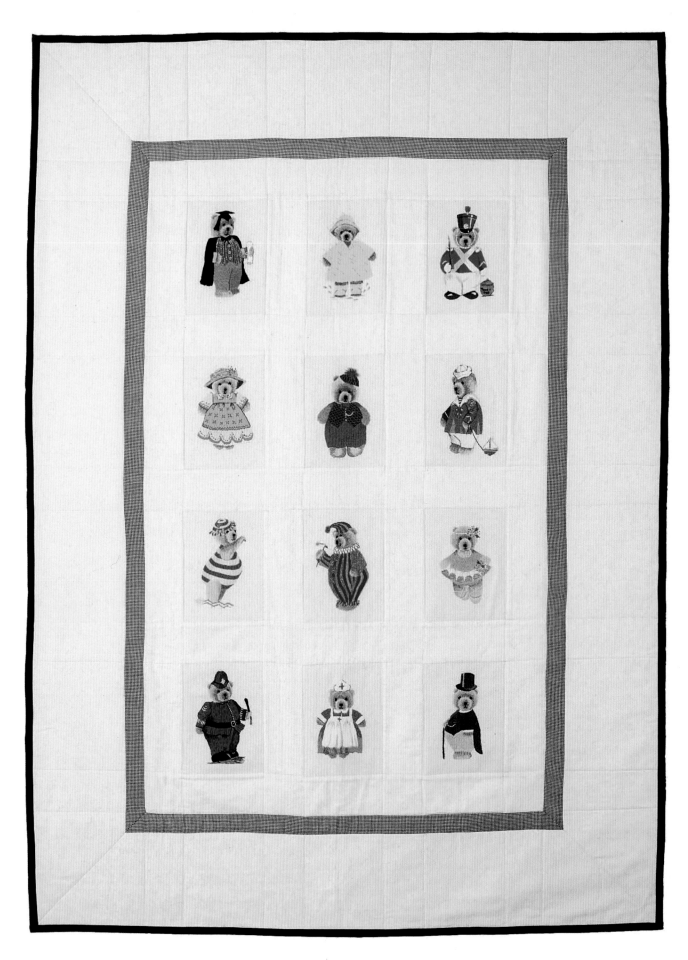

The quilt measures 182cm x 133cm wide (71 $\frac{1}{2}$" x 52 $\frac{1}{2}$")

FABRIC

60cm x 160cm wide
(24" x 1yd 27") of ivory wool
blanketing

5.8m x 122cm wide
(6yd 12 ½" x 48") of cream
100% cotton damask

2m x 30cm wide (2yd 6 ¾" x 12")
piece of black fine gingham

90cm x 112cm wide (35 ½" x 44")
black cotton homespun

1.5m x 210cm wide
(1yd 23" x 83") thin wool and
polyester blend wadding

THREADS & NEEDLES

See page 6.

SUPPLIES

13cm x 23cm (5" x 9") oval
embroidery hoop

1.5m x 50cm wide (1yd 4" x 20")
of water-soluble stabiliser
eg *Solvy*

100% cotton machine sewing
thread to match the damask

Black 100% cotton machine
sewing thread

30cm x 26cm wide (12 x 10 ¼")
piece of thin cardboard

Brown medium gel pen
eg *Sakura* gelly roll

Rotary cutter (optional)

Quilting safety pins (optional)

Walking foot to suit your sewing
machine (optional)

THIS DESIGN USES

~ Back stitch
~ Bullion knot
~ Chain stitch
~ Couching
~ Detached chain
~ Fly stitch
~ French knot

~ Ghiordes knot
~ Lattice couching
~ Satin stitch
~ Soft shading
~ Split stitch
~ Stem stitch
~ Straight stitch

THREADS AND NEEDLES

Fine 2ply wool

A = white
B = black
C = dk carnation
D = carnation
E = vy lt carnation
F = lt carnation
G = fuchsia
H = candy pink
I = burgundy
J = dk plum
K = plum
L = mahogany
M = med mahogany
N = lt rose pink
O = lt shell pink
P = vy lt shell pink
Q = ultra lt shell pink
R = Christmas red
S = lt flame red
T = med flame red

U = red
V = ultra lt terra cotta
W = dk antique blue
X = antique blue
Y = med blue
Z = dk electric blue
AA = med electric blue
AB = sky blue
AC = lt sky blue
AD = powder blue
AE = vy dk china blue
AF = med china blue
AG = vy lt china blue
AH = French navy
AI = peacock blue
AJ = steel grey
AK = dk beaver grey
AL = pearl grey
AM = dk blue-violet
AN = blue-violet
AO = dk purple
AP = vy lt purple
AQ = dk lavender
AR = lavender

AS = lt mauve
AT = vy dk flesh tint
AU = dk lemon
AV = med lemon
AW = lt lemon
AX = vy lt lemon
AY = egg yolk
AZ = autumn yellow
BA = lt autumn yellow
BB = bright yellow
BC = med bright yellow
BD = avocado
BE = med yellow-green
BF = golden olive
BG = vy dk olive green
BH = dk mustard
BI = dk fawn
BJ = tan
BK = dk chestnut
BL = ultra lt biscuit brown
BM = vy lt biscuit brown
BN = med biscuit brown
BO = lt mocha
BP = lt chocolate

BQ = chocolate
BR = golden brown

Blending filaments
BS = pearl
BT = confetti

Stranded metallic thread
BU = gold
BV = silver

Stranded rayon
BW = med violet
BX = lt plum

Stranded silk
BY = egg yolk
BZ = grey
CA = black
CB = white

Needles
No. 7 crewel
No. 9 crewel
No. 20 chenille

Preparation for embroidery

See pages 33 - 44 for the embroidery designs and stitch direction diagrams.

PREPARING THE FABRIC

Cut the blanketing into twelve pieces, each 30cm x 26cm wide (12" x 10¼").

Cut the water-soluble stabiliser into twelve pieces, each 25cm (10") square.

TRANSFERRING THE DESIGN

Using the gel pen, trace one bear design and grainline onto the water-soluble stabiliser.

Centre the tracing over a piece of blanketing, aligning the grainline with the straight grain of the fabric. Tack the tracing in place around the design.

The embroidery is stitched through all layers and the stabiliser dissolved once the embroidery is complete.

We recommend you complete the embroidery of each bear before transferring the next as the water-soluble stabiliser can become dry and rigid over time.

Embroidery

See pages 8 - 19 for instructions for each individual bear. See pages 24 - 32 for the step-by-step instructions for the embroidery stitches.

Use the chenille needle when stitching with the wool. Use the no. 9 crewel needle when stitching with one or two strands of thread and the no. 7 crewel needle when stitching with three to six strands.

Place the fabric in the hoop for all embroidery except stem stitch and fly stitch. Stab the needle up and down rather than skimming it from one stitch to the next. As you stitch support the fabric to prevent distortion and maintain even tension (diag 1). Do not pull stitches too tight.

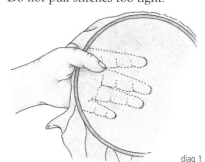

diag 1

ORDER OF WORK

For all designs, work the bear's head first. Each head is embroidered in the same manner, but using different coloured wools. Refer to each individual embroidery key for thread colours.

Complete the embroidery for each bear following the instructions given. When filling in larger areas in long and short stitch, begin by working directional lines using two strands of thread referring to the stitch direction diagram. Fill the shape using one strand.

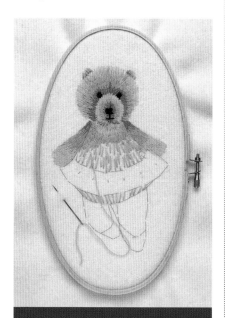

"Working the directional lines in two strands helps to quickly fill the larger areas. I do not recommend the whole item is done in this way as you do not achieve a smooth effect."
Jenny

Construction
See pages 21 - 23.

EMBROIDERING THE BEAR'S HEAD

We omitted the water-soluble stabiliser and used perlé cotton for photographic purposes.

1. Work the eyes and nose in satin stitch.

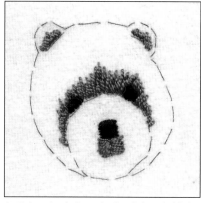

2. Using the darkest shade of thread, fill the inner ear, below the nose and around the eyes with long and short stitch.

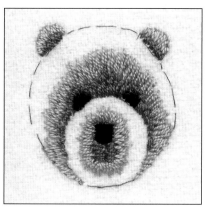

3. Change to the medium shade of thread. Using long and short stitch, fill the remainder of the ears, surround the stitching in the nose and mouth area and the inner section of the head.

4. Change to the lightest thread. Working from the previous stitching, fill the muzzle and then the remainder of the head with long and short stitch. Remove any tacking showing through the embroidery.

5. Stitch the mouth in back stitch over the previous stitching.

CLASS OF 99

THREADS & BUTTONS

B = black
K = plum
AJ = steel grey
AL = pearl grey
AP = vy lt purple
AS = lt mauve
AY = egg yolk
BL = ultra lt biscuit
BM = vy lt biscuit
BR = golden brown
BU = gold
BW = med violet
BX = lt plum
BZ = grey
CA = black
CB = white
3 x 6mm (1/4") pink doll buttons

EMBROIDERY KEY

All embroidery is worked with one strand unless otherwise specified.

Eyes and nose = B (satin stitch)

Mouth = B (back stitch, satin stitch)

Head, hands, ears and feet = BL
BM and BR (long and short stitch)

Cape = B
(1 - 2 strands, long and short stitch)

Bow tie = B
(satin stitch, straight stitch)
Outlines = AJ (straight stitch)

Mortar board = B
(1 - 2 strands, long and short stitch)
AJ (back stitch)

Tassel = CA
(2 strands, couching, whipping)

Shirt cuffs = AL (long and short stitch)
AJ (stem stitch, straight stitch)

Scroll = CB (3 strands, long and
short stitch), BZ (back stitch)

Bow = AY (6 strands, laid thread)
AY (couching)

Waistcoat = K
(1 - 2 strands, long and short stitch)
Quilting lines = BW and BX
(2 strands stem stitch), BU (stem stitch)
Outline = BX (stem stitch)

Trousers = AP and AS
(long and short stitch)
Outline = K (long and short stitch)

Stitch the bear's head, hands and feet, leaving space for the scroll to be worked later. Add tiny satin stitches to the mouth. Work the hands and feet.

Embroider the cape, working long straight stitches that follow the stitch direction lines in two strands. Fill in with one strand. Stitch the bow tie and the mortar board. Partially outline them with steel grey wool.

To form the tassel, cut three lengths of black silk thread, each 6cm (2 3/8") long. Lay the cut lengths of thread on the hat so that the centre of the threads align with the top of the tassel indicated on the design. Using two strands of thread, couch the cut lengths in place at the centre. Fold the cut lengths together. Using the couching thread, whip the top 6mm (1/4").

Take the thread through the wrapping and work one to two tiny back stitches to finish off. Trim the tails of silk so they are even.

Embroider the shirt cuffs using two shades of grey wool. Stitch the scroll with the white silk. Form a bow with six strands of yellow silk and couch in place. Outline the scroll with one strand of grey silk.

Stitch the waistcoat in long and short stitch and then the rows of quilting in stem stitch, alternating between shades of plum, gold and violet. Follow the contours of his very proud chest. Work the trousers in the same manner as the cape, adding a darker line between the legs. Outline the lower edge of the waistcoat in stem stitch and attach the three buttons.

SPLASH

THREADS

B = black
U = red
AC = lt sky blue
AJ = steel grey
AL = pearl grey
AU = dk lemon
BC = med bright yellow
BO = lt mocha
BP = lt chocolate
BQ = chocolate

EMBROIDERY KEY

All embroidery is worked with one strand unless otherwise specified.

Eyes and nose = B (satin stitch)

Mouth = B (back stitch)

Head = BO, BP and BQ
(2 strands, long and short stitch)

Hands = BP and BQ
(long and short stitch)

Knees = BP and BQ (straight stitch)

Sou'wester = AJ, AU and BC
(long and short stitch)

Outlines = AJ and AL
(stem stitch, straight stitch)

Scarf = U (2 strands, long and short stitch)

Raincoat = AU and BC
(1 - 2 strands, long and short stitch)

Pocket = AU (satin stitch)

Collar = AU (long and short stitch)

Gum boots = AJ, AU and BC
(long and short stitch)

Outlines = AJ (stem stitch, straight stitch)

Rain, puddle and splashes
= AC (straight stitch)

Embroider the bear's head following the general instructions, omitting the ears. Stitch the hands and knees.

Work the sou'wester following the stitch direction diagram. Fill in the inside of the hat. Partially outline the brim with two strands of grey.

Embroider the red scarf in long and short stitch. Using two strands of wool, randomly cover the raincoat with long straight stitches that follow the stitch direction lines, omitting the collar and pocket. Change to one strand of wool and complete the raincoat, again omitting the collar and pocket.

Stitch the pocket in satin stitch and the collar in long and short stitch.

Work the gum boots using the darker shade of yellow for the toe area and the lighter shade of yellow for the top of the boots and the highlight on the toes. Stitch the soles in long and short stitch and partially outline the top and toe of each boot in stem stitch.

Scatter straight stitches for the rain, then form each splash with five to six stitches in the shape of an upside down teardrop (diag 2). Work the puddles in straight stitch.

diag 2

HALT! WHO GOES THERE

THREADS

A = white
B = black
I = burgundy
L = mahogany
R = Christmas red
X = antique blue
Z = dk electric blue
AA = med electric blue
AD = powder blue
AH = French navy
AI = peacock blue
AJ = steel grey
AL = lt sky blue
AM = dk blue-violet
BF = golden olive
BI = dk fawn
BK = dk chestnut
BL = ultra lt biscuit
BM = vy lt biscuit
BP = lt chocolate
BR = golden brown
BU = gold
BX = lt plum

EMBROIDERY KEY

All embroidery is worked with one strand unless otherwise specified.

Eyes and nose = B (satin stitch)

Mouth = B (back stitch)

Ears = BM and BR (long and short stitch)

Head = BL, BM and BR
(long and short stitch)

Tunic = I and R
(1 - 2 strands, long and short stitch)

Outlines = AH (back stitch)

Rank markings = A
(stem stitch, straight stitch)

Chest straps = A and AD
(long and short stitch)

Chest straps outlines = I (stem stitch)

Collar = BU
(2 strands, long and short stitch)

Epaulets = BU (2 strands, straight stitch)

Trousers = A and AD
(1 - 2 strands, long and short stitch)

Outlines = AD and AJ (stem stitch)

Gloves = A
(2 strands, long and short stitch)
AH and AJ (back stitch, straight stitch)

Shoes = AI and X
(1 - 2 strands, long and short stitch, stem stitch), A (2 strands, long and short stitch)

Hat = A, X, Z, AA and AM
(long and short stitch, straight stitch)
Outlines = AH (straight stitch)
AA (stem stitch)
Braid on peak = BU (2 strands, stem stitch)
Chin strap = BU (2 strands, chain stitch)
Badge = BU (6 strands, laid thread)
BX (couching)

Plume = R and AJ (straight stitch)
BU (3 strands, 3 French knots, 1 wrap)

Honey pot = BF, BI and BP
(long and short stitch)
Outline = BI and BK (back stitch)
Letters = B (back stitch)

Rifle = L and BK (long and short stitch)
AH (stem stitch)

Bayonet = AC
(long and short stitch, straight stitch)

Embroider the bear's head and ears. Work the tunic and stitch the white sleeve markings. Outline the chest straps with burgundy and fill in with long and short stitch, using the powder blue wool on the left and the white wool on the right side.

Stitch the trousers, working direction lines with two strands of wool. Fill in using one strand. Stitch the gloves and shoes, adding highlights to the shoes with two strands of white wool.

Fill in the hat following the divisions on the design. Partially outline the top and right hand side. Mark the division above the peak in stem stitch. Add markings across the top of the hat. Work the plume on the hat with uneven straight stitches. Shade with six to seven stitches in steel grey.

Stitch gold French knots on the plume and couch a spiral of laid thread for the badge, working approximately three rounds. Embroider the braid around the peak of the hat and the chin strap. Work the collar and finish the jacket with gold epaulets.

Embroider the honey pot in long and short stitch and outline it with a combination of straight stitch and stem stitch. Work the shadow below the pot in straight stitch and form the letters with back stitch.

Work the rifle and bayonet, carefully following the design. When outlining the rifle also partially outline the gloves, shoes and sleeve on the right side.

SUNDAY BEST

EMBROIDERY KEY

All embroidery is worked with one strand unless otherwise specified.

Eyes and nose = B (satin stitch)

Mouth = B (back stitch)

Head and hands = L, M and BJ
(2 strands, long and short stitch)

Feet = L and M
(2 strands, long and short stitch)

DRESS

Collar = A (satin stitch)

Outline = AJ (back stitch)

Dress = AW and AX
(1 - 2 strands, long and short stitch)

Cuffs and hem = BF (satin stitch)
BG (French knot, 1 - 2 wraps)

Outline = BG (stem stitch, back stitch)

Apron = BE
(1 - 2 strands, long and short stitch)

Fabric design and border = A and BG
(straight stitch)

Outline = BG (stem stitch, back stitch)

Gathers = BG (2 strands, straight stitch)

Petticoat = A (French knot, 2 wraps)

HAT

Underside of brim = BK (2 strands long and short stitch, back stitch)

Brim = AZ, BA and BB (stem stitch)

Crown = AZ, BA and BB
(long and short stitch)

Wicker weaving = BN
(2 strands, straight stitch)

Ears = M (2 strands, straight stitch)

FLOWERS

Rose centre = D
(3 - 4 bullion knots, 5 wraps)

Petals = E (satin stitch straight stitch)

Leaves = BD
(detached chain)

Buds = G
(French knot
1 - 2 wraps)

Embroider the bear's head following the instructions on page 7, omitting the ears. Work the hands and feet, grading from the darkest shade at the top, to the lightest shade at the ends.

Embroider the collar of the dress in white. Stitch the sleeves and lower skirt in light lemon, working the stitch direction lines in two strands and filling in with long and short stitch using one strand. Fill the area around the collar with very light lemon long and short stitches. Stitch the cuffs and hem in a scallop pattern. Add French knot spots above the scallops. Embroider the apron in the same manner as the dress. Work straight stitches to form the gathers. Stitch the dark green design on the apron

diag 3

with crossed straight stitches, each anchored at the centre (diag 3). Embroider the hem design on the apron in a similar manner. Anchor each cross with a horizontal straight stitch. Partially outline the sleeves, collar and apron. Add a petticoat frill of white French knots.

Embroider the straw hat starting with the underside of the brim. Stitch the top of the brim and crown following the stitch direction diagram and noting the colour changes. Work the wicker weaving lines over the brim and crown in straight stitch. Stitch the ears just peeking from the sides of the hat.

To finish, work a rose, flower buds and leaves on the collar and hat.

BOOK WORM

THREADS

B = black
J = dk plum
AM = dk blue-violet
AQ = dk lavender
BO = lt mocha
BP = lt chocolate
BQ = chocolate
BU = gold

EMBROIDERY KEY

All embroidery is worked with one strand unless otherwise specified.

Eyes and nose = B (satin stitch)

Mouth = B (2 strands, back stitch)

Head = BO, BP and BQ
(1 - 2 strands, long and short stitch)

Ear and arms = BP and BQ
(1 - 2 strands, long and short stitch)

Feet = BP and BQ
(1 - 2 strands, long and short stitch)

Feet outlines = BQ (stem stitch)

Waistcoat = J (1 - 2 strands, long and short stitch), AQ (lattice couching)

Outlines = AM and AQ (stem stitch)

Pocket = AQ (straight stitch)

Watch chain = BU (2 strands, chain stitch)

Buttons = BU
(2 strands, French knot, 1 wrap)

Eye glasses = BU
(2 strands, back stitch, stem stitch)

Bow tie loops = AM and AQ
(straight stitch)

Knot = AQ (satin stitch)

Cap = J (1 - 2 strands, long and short stitch), AM (lattice couching)

Pompom = AM (ghiordes knot)

Trousers = AM
(1 - 2 strands, long and short stitch)

Highlights = AQ
(1 - 2 strands, long and short stitch)

Stitch the bear's head, using one to two strands of each wool. Work the ear and arms. Embroider the feet with the two lighter shades and partially outline them with the darkest shade.

Embroider the waistcoat leaving space for the bow tie. Using the dark lavender wool, work long diagonal straight stitches approximately 5mm (3/16") apart over one side of the waistcoat. Then work long diagonal stitches in the opposite direction. Where the diagonal lines meet, work a tiny couching stitch to hold them in place. Work the other side in the same manner. Outline the lower and centre front edges of the waistcoat in stem stitch, changing the colour of the lower outline for the bear's left hand side of the waistcoat. Work two straight stitches very close together for the top of the pocket. Stitch the gold fob watch chain from the pocket to the centre front of the vest. Add six French knot buttons to the waistcoat.

Work the eye glasses, then embroider the bow tie. Work the bow loops first and then the knot. Stitch the cap using the same method as the waistcoat. Work a pompom with ghiordes knots.

Using two strands, partially fill the trousers following the stitch direction lines. Fill in with one strand adding shading with the lighter colour.

SHIP AHOY

THREADS

A = white
B = black
C = dk carnation
I = burgundy
N = lt rose pink
S = lt flame red
T = med flame red
U = red
AC = lt sky blue
AD = powder blue
AE = vy dk china blue
AF = med china blue
AG = vy lt china blue
AH = French navy
AJ = steel grey
AK = dk beaver grey
AT = vy dk flesh tint
AY = egg yolk
BH = dk mustard
BU = gold

EMBROIDERY KEY

All embroidery is worked with one strand unless otherwise specified.

Eyes and nose = B (satin stitch)

Mouth = B (back stitch)

Head = S, T and AT (long and short stitch)

Hands = S, T and AT (long and short stitch)

Feet = N, S, T, and AT (long and short stitch)

Claws = AT (straight stitch)

Hat = A, AC and AD (long and short stitch)

Button = AC (straight stitch)
A (French knot, 2 wraps)

Outlines and highlights = AC, AD and AK (straight stitch), AD (stem stitch)

Anchor badge = BU
(2 strands, straight stitch, couching)

Collar = A and AD (long and short stitch)

Outlines = AE and AF (back stitch)

Braid = U (back stitch)

T-shirt = A and AE (satin stitch)

Jacket = AE, AF and AG
(1 - 2 strands, long and short stitch)

Outlines = AE and AJ
(stem stitch, straight stitch, back stitch)

Piping on cuffs = A (split stitch)

Rank stripes = U and C (straight stitch)

Buttons = BU
(2 strands, French knot, 1 wrap)

Anchor = BU
(2 strands, straight stitch, couching)

Bow = I, U and C (satin stitch
straight stitch), A (straight stitch)

Trousers = A and AD
(1 - 2 strands, long and short stitch)

Outlines = AJ and AD
(stem stitch, straight stitch)

BOAT

Hull = U
(long and short stitch, straight stitch)

Hull stripe = AY (stem stitch)

Mast = BH (stem stitch)

Flag = AY (satin stitch)

Sails = A (long and short stitch)

Outlines = AD and AJ
(straight stitch, stem stitch, back stitch)

Wheel = BH (satin stitch)
AH (French knot), AJ (back stitch)

String = AH (stem stitch)

Embroider the bear's head and ears following the instructions on page 7. Once the head is complete, stitch the hands and feet.

Work the hat in long and short stitch and partially outline in back stitch. Stitch a triangle of three straight stitches for the button at the top. Add a French knot in the middle. Embroider the collar in long and short stitch. Work the t-shirt with white and blue straight stitch stripes. Using back stitch, partially outline the bear's right hand collar neckline in AF and the left hand collar neckline in AE. Embroider the red braid on the lower edge of the collar.

Using two strands of wool, randomly cover the sailor suit jacket with straight stitches that follow the stitch direction diagram. Change to one strand and then complete the jacket. Embroider a gold anchor on the hat and sleeve in straight stitch, couching along the curve. Add the buttons with French knots. Stitch the bow, following the stitch direction diagram and noting the colour changes.

Work the trousers in long and short stitch and partially outline the legs. Work the hands and feet in long and short stitch, beginning with the darkest thread and grading to the lightest. Add straight stitch claws to the bear's left hand.

Stitch the boat hull with horizontal long and short stitches. Add a yellow stripe. Embroider the mast, flag and sails. Work the outline in back stitch and add a French knot for the centre. Embroider the navy rope in stem stitch.

BATHING BEAUTY

THREADS

A = white
B = black
C = dk carnation
F = lt carnation
L = mahogany
M = med mahogany
AB = sky blue
AM = dk blue-violet
AQ = dk lavender
AV = med lemon
AX = vy lt lemon
BJ = tan
BV = silver

EMBROIDERY KEY

All embroidery is worked with one strand unless otherwise specified.

Eyes and nose = B (satin stitch)

Mouth = B (back stitch)

Head, arm, paws and legs = L, M and BJ (long and short stitch)

Arm outline = M (stem stitch)

Ears = L (satin stitch)

Bathing costume = AQ and AV (1 - 2 strands, long and short stitch)

Highlights = AM and AX (long and short stitch)

HAT

Crown = AQ and AV (long and short stitch)

Frill = AQ and AV (satin stitch)

Bow loops = C and F (long and short stitch)

Bow knot = F (satin stitch)

Water = A, AB and BV (straight stitch)

Sand = AV (straight stitch)

Embroider the bear's head, ears, arm, paws and legs, grading the thread colours referring to the embroidery design and photograph.

Work the crown of the hat, starting at the base and working towards the top. Stitch the frill using two to six straight stitches for each stripe. Embroider the bow loops in long and short stitch and the bow knot in satin stitch. Add the band in stem stitch.

Embroider the bear's bathing costume working in a similar manner to the crown of the hat. In the area between the arm and the leg, blend the threads in each stripe to create the highlighted area which is a water reflection.

Embroider water around the bear's knees. Let the stitches for the water be uneven as they represent choppy waves. Add silver straight stitches for water sparkle.

Work straight stitches of varying lengths in medium lemon next to the water for sand.

"When working the frill it is not necessary to make the stripes identical, as this is supposed to look like gathered fabric and does not need to look regimented."
Jenny

CLOWNING AROUND

THREADS

A = white
B = black
G = fuchsia
H = candy pink
AI = peacock blue
AJ = steel grey
AK = dk beaver grey
AN = blue-violet
AO = dk purple
AY = egg yolk
BG = vy dk olive green
BH = dk mustard
BL = ultra lt biscuit
BM = vy lt biscuit
BN = med biscuit
BS = pearl
BT = confetti

EMBROIDERY KEY

All embroidery is worked with one strand unless otherwise specified.

Eyes and nose = B (satin stitch)

Mouth = B (back stitch)

Head, ears and hands = BL, BM and BN (long and short stitch)

Feet = BM and BN (long and short stitch)

Collar = A and BS (1 strand of each straight stitch), AK (back stitch)

Hat = AI, AN and AO (long and short stitch), G and BT (1 strand of each, long and short stitch)

Overalls = AI, AN and AO (long and short stitch), G and BT (1 strand of each, long and short stitch)

Right arm = AI, AN and AO (long and short stitch), G and BT (1 strand of each, long and short stitch)

Left arm = G and BT (1 strand of each, long and short stitch)

Outlines and crease lines = H (back stitch, straight stitch)

Frill = AI and AO (straight stitch) G and BT (1 strand of each, straight stitch)

Pompoms = G and BT (1 strand of each, ghiordes knot)

FLOWER

Stem = BG (stem stitch)

Leaf = BG (straight stitch)

Centre = BH (straight stitch)

Petals = AY (straight stitch)

Embroider the bear's head following the instructions on page 7. Using long and short stitch, work the hands, ears and feet, referring to the photograph for colour placement.

Work the collar, outlining the frill in small back stitches. Fill each section of the frill with straight stitches.

Stitch the clown's hat following the stitch direction lines and noting the changes of colour. The fuchsia stripe is worked with one strand of wool and one strand of the blending filament.

Embroider the body of the overalls and the bear's right arm in the same manner as the hat. The frills at the ankles are worked with three to six stitches in the shape of a tear-drop. Fill in any gaps with the dark purple thread, giving the effect of a ruffled frill.

Work the bear's left arm and outline the lower edge of the sleeve and crease lines in the darker pink.

Form each of the four pompoms with ghiordes knots.

Stitch the flower in the bear's hand using stem stitch for the stem and straight stitch for the flower and leaf.

DANCING QUEEN

THREADS

A = white
B = black
D = carnation
F = lt carnation
L = mahogany
M = med mahogany
O = lt shell pink
P = vy lt shell pink
Q = ultra lt shell pink
AL = pearl grey
AR = lavender
BD = avocado
BJ = tan

EMBROIDERY KEY

All embroidery is worked with one strand unless otherwise specified.

Eyes and nose = B (satin stitch)

Mouth = B (back stitch)

Ears = L and M (long and short stitch)

Head, arms, chest and legs = BJ, L and M (long and short stitch)

Leotard = AR
(1 - 2 strands, long and short stitch)

Pearls = A
(2 strands, French knot, 2 wraps)

Tutu = A (long and short stitch)
AL (straight stitch)

Border = O (French knot, 1 - 2 wraps)

Outline = A (straight stitch)

Ballet shoes = P and Q
(long and short stitch)

Outlines = O (stem stitch)

Ribbons = Q (2 strands, split stitch)
A (whipping)

FLOWERS

Rose centre = O (satin stitch)

Petals = F (2 strands, straight stitch)

Leaves = BD (fly stitch)

Buds = BD (French knot, 1 - 2 wraps)

Head band = A (2 strands, split stitch)

Embroider the bear's head referring to the instructions on page 7. Work the arms and legs, grading from the darkest shade at the top, to the lightest shade at the ends. Fill the ears and chest with long and short stitch.

Work the leotard, first stitching the stitch direction lines in two strands and filling with long and short stitch using one strand. Embroider the pearls around the neck of the leotard with white French knots.

Work the tutu in long and short stitch. To achieve the gathered effect on the tutu, stitch groups of three straight stitches along the upper edge. Fill the scallops with pink French knots for the border design. Outline the top of the tutu with a series of straight stitches.

Stitch the ballet shoes with long and short stitch and the ribbons using whipped split stitch. Outline the top of the shoes in stem stitch.

Embroider the flowers with satin stitch centres surrounded by overlapping straight stitches. Add fly stitch leaves and a sprinkling of French knots. The white headband is worked in split stitch.

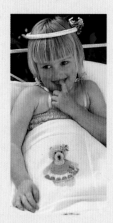

HELLO HELLO HELLO

THREADS

A = white
B = black
L = mahogany
W = dk antique blue
X = antique blue
Y = med blue
AJ = steel grey
BK = dk chestnut
BL = ultra lt biscuit
BM = vy lt biscuit
BR = golden brown
BV = silver

EMBROIDERY KEY

All embroidery is worked with one strand unless otherwise specified.

Eyes and nose = B (satin stitch)

Mouth = B (back stitch)

Head and hands = BL, BM and BR (long and short stitch)

Ears = BM and BR (long and short stitch)

Jacket and trousers = W and Y (1 - 2 strands, long and short stitch) X (straight stitch)

Left hand arm band = A and W (straight stitch)

Right hand arm band = A and X (straight stitch)

Rank stripes = A (straight stitch)

Number badge = BV (2 strands, straight stitch)

Outline = B (stem stitch)

Collar = X (satin stitch) BV (2 strands, straight stitch)

Buttons = BV (2 strands, French knot)

Belt = B (long and short stitch)

Belt buckle = BV (2 strands, straight stitch)

Boots = B and AJ (long and short stitch) A and AJ (straight stitch)

Laces = B (back stitch)

Helmet = X and Y (long and short stitch)

Band = B (stem stitch)

Top crest = BV (2 strands, straight stitch)

Badge = BV (6 strands, laid thread couching; 2 strands, straight stitch)

Truncheon = B (long and short stitch, loop stitch)

Cobble stones = BK and L (straight stitch)

Embroider the bear's head, ears and hands following the instructions on page 7. Stitch the jacket and trousers using the same method as the cape in Class of 99. To achieve the look of thick woollen fabric, add random straight stitches in antique blue. Work the armband stripes in straight stitch, then the rank stripes on the sleeve. Work the belt in long and short stitch. Using black wool partially outline the jacket in stem stitch.

Stitch the black boots and add steel grey soles. Work white and steel grey highlights to the toes and stitch the black shoe laces in back stitch.

Embroider the helmet in long and short stitch, adding the black band in stem stitch.

Add the truncheon in long and short stitch. Form the strap on the handle with a small thread loop.

Using the silver metallic thread, work the buttons in French knots and the buckle, number badge and collar markings with straight stitch. On the helmet add a top crest and stitch the badge as for the badge on Halt! Who Goes There, adding four straight stitch arrows.

Work the cobble stones in uneven straight stitch.

FLORENCE

THREADS

A = white
B = black
S = lt flame red
T = med flame red
U = red
V = ultra lt terra cotta
AF = med china blue
AG = vy lt china blue
AJ = steel grey
AL = pearl grey
AT = vy dk flesh tint
BU = gold

EMBROIDERY KEY

All embroidery is worked with one strand unless otherwise specified.

Eyes and nose = B (satin stitch)

Mouth = B (2 strands, back stitch)

Head = S, V and AT
(long and short stitch)

Ears = S and V (long and short stitch)

Hands and feet = S and T
(long and short stitch)

Cap = A
(1 - 2 strands, long and short stitch)

Outline = AJ
(stem stitch, long and short stitch)

Dress = AF and AG
(1 - 2 strands, long and short stitch)

Cuffs = A (long and short stitch)

Cap and cuff outlines = AJ
(stem stitch, straight stitch)

Collar = A (satin stitch)

Buttons = BU
(2 strands, French knot, 1 wrap)

Apron = A and AL
(1 - 2 strands, long and short stitch)

Watch = BU (2 strands, satin stitch)

Watch chain = BU
(2 strands, chain stitch)

Red crosses = U
(2 strands, straight stitch)

Embroider the bear's head following the instructions on page 7. Stitch the ears, hands and feet, following the photograph and embroidery design for colour placement. Embroider the cap, working the stitch direction lines in two strands and filling in with long and short stitch using one strand.

Embroider the dress in the very light and medium bright china blue wools. Embroider the cuffs and apron in white wool. Shade the apron with pearl grey. Embroider the collar in satin stitch.

Outline the lower edge of the sleeve cuffs and partially outline the cap in steel grey.

Add a red cross to the apron bodice and to the cap. Stitch three buttons and the nurse's watch with the gold thread. Work the watch in satin stitch and the chain in chain stitch.

SQUIRE

THREADS

A = white
B = black
I = burgundy
L = mahogany
M = med mahogany
AJ = steel grey
AK = dk beaver grey
AL = pearl grey
BJ = tan
BU = gold

EMBROIDERY KEY

All embroidery is worked with one strand unless otherwise specified.

Eyes and nose = B (satin stitch)

Mouth = B (2 strands, back stitch)

Head, hands and feet = L, M and BJ
(1 - 2 strands, long and short stitch)

Ears = L and M (long and short stitch)

Jacket = AK
(1 - 2 strands, long and short stitch)

Sleeve and tails outline = B
(stem stitch, straight stitch)

Lapel outline = B and AJ
(2 strands, straight stitch)

Pocket = B and AJ
(2 strands, straight stitch)

Collar = A (stem stitch, straight stitch)

Cuffs = A (long and short stitch)

Cravat = I (long and short stitch)

Watch chain = BU (2 strands, chain stitch)

Trousers = AL (1 - 2 strands,
long and short stitch)

Top hat = B, AJ, AK and AL
(long and short stitch)

Outlines = B (stem stitch), AK (back stitch)

Walking stick = B and AK
(2 strands, split stitch)

Embroider the bear's head, ears, hands and feet. Stitch the jacket and trousers in long and short stitch. Leave a space for the shirt collar and cuff. Outline the tails and sleeve with black. Work the lapel outline and pocket in black and grey straight stitches. Add a gold watch chain.

Stitch the collar in stem stitch and straight stitch. Work the sleeve cuff in a horizontal band of long and short stitch. Change the direction of the long and short stitch and embroider the squire's cravat in burgundy.

Stitch the top hat using black and three shades of grey.

Add the walking stick using one row of black split stitch and one row of beaver grey split stitch.

OTHER IDEAS FOR THESE VERSATILE DESIGNS
Framed pictures for a nursery or a child's room, baby bags, bibs and pockets on pinafores or pants.

REQUIREMENTS

For full details, see pages 5 and 6.

PREPARATION FOR EMBROIDERY

For full instructions, see page 6.

EMBROIDERY

For full instructions, see pages 7 - 19.

CUTTING OUT

Cut out all pieces following the cutting layouts and using the measurements given below.

Cotton damask

Backing: cut two,
each 150cm x 100cm wide (59" x 39 1/2")

Sashing around bears: cut sixteen,
each 25cm x 10cm wide (9 3/4" x 4")
and five, each 10cm x 85cm wide (4" x 34")

Wide border: cut two,
each 190cm x 26cm wide (75" x 10 1/8")
and two, each 140cm x 26cm wide (55 1/2" x 10 1/8")

Black fine gingham

Inner border: cut two,
each 190cm x 6cm wide (75" x 2 3/8")
and two, each 140cm x 6cm wide (55 1/2" x 2 3/8")

Black cotton

Binding: cut four,
each 10cm x 98cm wide (4" x 38 1/2")
and four, each 10cm x 72cm wide (4" x 28 1/2")

Wadding

Cut one 150cm x 195cm wide (59" x 77")

CUTTING LAYOUTS

Cotton damask

1. Backing
2. Vertical sashing
3. Horizontal sashing
4. Vertical border
5. Horizontal border

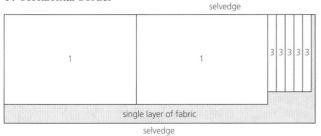

Black fine gingham

6. Vertical inner border
7. Horizontal inner border

Black cotton

8. Binding

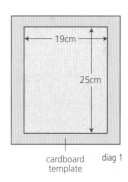

CONSTRUCTION

All seam allowances are 1cm (3/8") unless otherwise specified. The shaded areas on the following diagrams indicate the right side of the fabric. Refer to the placement diagram for the positions of the bears, sashing and border strips. Use the quilting diagram as a guide when stitching the rows of quilting.

1. Preparation

For each embroidered bear piece, remove any tacking threads still showing through the embroidery. Place the embroidered pieces face down onto a well padded surface and press.

Make a window template by cutting out a 25cm x 19cm wide (9 3/4" x 7 1/2") section from the centre of the thin cardboard (*diag 1*).

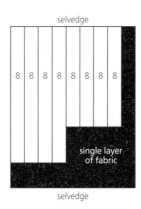

diag 1

Place the window template over the right side of one of the bears. Ensure the grain of the fabric aligns with the template edges and the bear is centred within the window. Trace around the inside edge of the template with the tailor's chalk. Cut out along the traced lines. Repeat for the remaining bears. To indicate the corners of the stitch lines, mark four points 1cm (3/8") in from each edge at the corners by stitching a piece of black sewing cotton through the wool blanketing (*diag 2*).

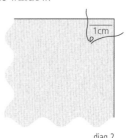

diag 2

Use the thread marks as guides when sewing the embroidered pieces to the sashing.

2. Piecing the bears into horizontal rows

With right sides together, pin and stitch one short piece of sashing lengthwise to the left hand side of the Class of 99 bear (*diag 3*).

Join the second short strip to the right hand side of this bear in the same manner (*diag 4*).

Using a pressing cloth and working on a well padded surface, carefully press the seams away from the bear on the wrong side of the fabric.

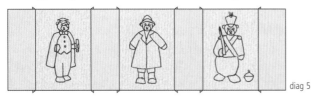

Join Splash, Halt Who Goes There and two more pieces of sashing, using the same method as before (*diag 5*).

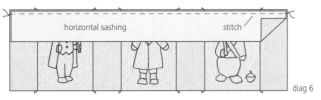

Form the remaining three rows of bears in the same manner.

3. Joining the horizontal rows

With right sides together, pin and stitch one long sashing strip to the top edge of the first row of bears (*diag 6*).

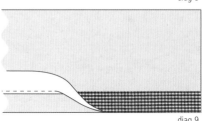

Press the seam away from the bears as before.

Attach a second piece of sashing to the lower edge of the bears in the same manner (*diag 7*).

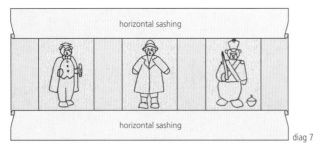

Join the remaining rows of bears and sashings together to complete the centre panel. Take special care to align the vertical seam lines.

4. Gingham borders

With the sharp pencil or fabric marker, mark the right side of one piece of the damask vertical border 4cm (1 $^5/_8$") in from one raw edge. With right sides together, pin the corresponding gingham fabric to the damask, aligning the raw edge of the gingham with the marked line (*diag 8*).

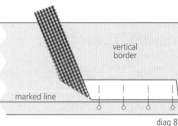

Stitch along the stitch line. Aligning raw edges, fold the gingham fabric back along the stitch line to cover the seam allowance Press. This now becomes the inner edge of the border (*diag 9*).

Baste the check fabric to the damask along the raw edges. Repeat for the remaining vertical border and both horizontal borders.

5. Marking centres

Fold the centre panel into quarters. Mark each fold at the outer edge to mark the centre of each side. Fold each border strip in half. Mark the fold at the inner edge of the border.

6. Forming the mitred border

With right sides together and matching centre marks, pin the inner edge of one border piece to the corresponding outer edge of the centre panel. The border will extend by approximately 28cm (11") beyond the ends of the centre panel. Beginning and ending lcm ($^3/_8$") from the sides of the centre panel, stitch the border piece in place (*diag 10*).

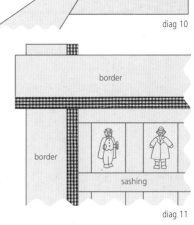

Finish off the ends securely. Repeat for the remaining border pieces. Press the border pieces away from the centre panel (*diag 11*).

Starting at one corner and with right sides together, fold the centre panel diagonally so the inner and outer edges of the two adjacent border pieces are aligned. Rule a diagonal line from the junction of the stitching lines at the corner of the

centre panel and finish at the
raw ends of the border. Ensure
the line is placed at 45° to the
outer edge. Pin and stitch along
the marked line (*diag 12*).

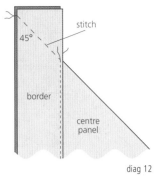

diag 12

Trim away the excess fabric
along the diagonal seam,
leaving a 1cm (³/8") seam
allowance. Press the seam
open. Repeat for each of the
remaining corners.

7. Piecing the backing

With right sides together and raw edges even, pin and stitch
the two backing pieces together along their longer sides. This
will make a piece 198cm x 150cm (78" x 59").

8. Assembling the layers

Evenly lay the backing fabric on a smooth, flat surface with
the right side facing down. Centre the wadding over the
backing, smoothing out from the centre. With the right side
facing up, centre the quilt top
over the wadding. The top is
smaller than the wadding and
backing. Carefully smooth the
top, taking care not to distort the
fabric. Starting at the centre and
using quilting pins or a needle
and sewing thread, pin or tack
the layers together. Continue to
smooth the top as you go. Work
towards the outer edges,
ensuring that the quilting pins or
the tacking lines are approx
10cm (4") apart (*diag 13*).

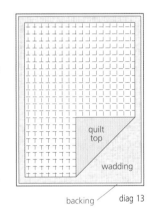

diag 13

Tack around the edges of the quilt top.

9. Quilting the layers

For best results use an even feed, or walking foot attachment
on your sewing machine. This produces a more even stitch
and also helps to avoid puckering of the fabric along the
stitchline. Use a stitch length of approximately 3 - 4mm
(³/16"), securing the stitching at the beginning and end of each
row. Roll the quilt edges in to keep the quilt to a manageable
size. Following the quilting
stitch guide and starting near
the centre, 'stitch in the
ditch' along all the joins.
Extend the stitching across
the damask where indicated
to form the squares between
the corners of each panel.
Rows of stitching are also
worked from the outer edge
of the gingham border to the
edge of the quilt (*diag 14*).

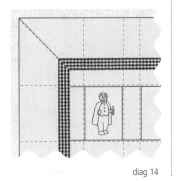

diag 14

10. Binding the quilt

Join two long strips to form one vertical binding. Repeat for
the two remaining long strips. For the horizontal bindings,
join the short strips in a similar manner. With wrong sides
together, fold one of the vertical sections in half along the
length. Press.

Beginning on one long side and aligning the raw edges of the
double binding with the raw edges of the damask border, pin
and stitch through all layers 1cm (³/8") in from the raw edge
(*diag 15*).

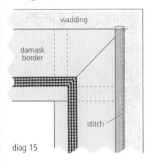
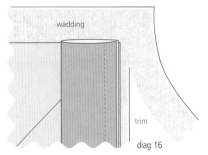

diag 15   diag 16

Trim away the excess wadding and backing along the long
side leaving a 19mm (³/4") seam allowance (*diag 16*).

Repeat for the remaining vertical side. Fold the binding over
the seam allowance and to the back of the quilt on each side.
Hand stitch the binding to the previous stitchline (*diag 17*).

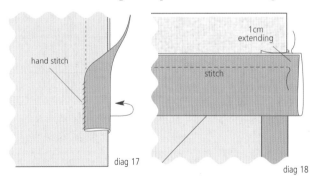

diag 17   diag 18

With right sides together, press the two remaining pieces of
binding in half along the length. With 1cm (³/8") of the binding extending at the beginning, pin one piece of double binding
along one end of the quilt. Stitch. Trim any excess length of
binding allowing 1cm (³/8") to extend at the end (*diag 18*).

Trim away the excess wadding and backing as before. Fold in
the raw ends and then fold the binding over to the wrong
side. Hand stitch the
binding and the corners
in place using small
stitches (*diag 19*).

Repeat for the remaining
end of the quilt.

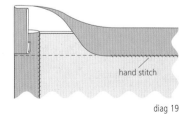

diag 19

11. Finishing

Remove all tacking threads and any remaining quilting pins.
If necessary, press carefully from the back.

BACK STITCH

Back stitch can be worked by either skimming the needle through the fabric while holding it freely in your hand as shown here, or by stabbing the needle up and down with the fabric held taut in a hoop or frame.

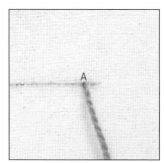

1. Mark a line on the fabric. Bring the thread to the front at A, a short distance from the right hand end of the marked line.

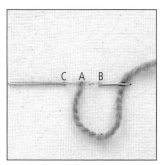

2. Take the needle to the back at B, at the beginning of the marked line. Emerge at C. The distance from A to C should be the same as the distance from A to B.

3. Pull the thread through.

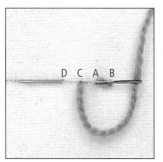

4. Take the needle to the back at A, through the same hole in the fabric. Emerge at D. The distance from C to D is the same as from A to C.

5. Continue working stitches in the same manner, keeping them all the same length.

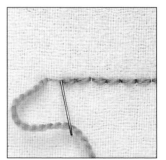

6. To finish, take the needle to the back of the fabric through the hole at the beginning of the previous stitch. Pull the thread through and end off.

BULLION KNOT

Bullion knots have been used in many forms of embroidery through the ages and are known by various names. These include grub stitch, caterpillar stitch, coil stitch, knot stitch, post stitch, roll stitch, worm stitch and Porto Rico rose.

The distance from A to B is the length of the finished bullion knot. To form a straight knot the number of wraps must cover this distance plus an extra 1 - 2 wraps.

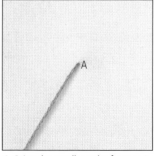

1. Bring the needle to the front at A. Pull the thread through.

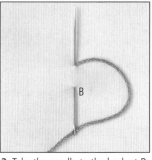

2. Take the needle to the back at B. Re-emerge at A, taking care not to split the thread. The thread is to the right of the needle.

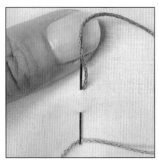

3. Raise the point of the needle away from the fabric. Wrap the thread clockwise around the needle.

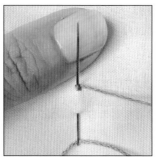

4. Keeping the point of the needle raised, pull the wrap firmly down onto the fabric.

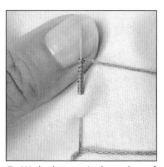

5. Work the required number of wraps around the needle. Pack them down evenly as you wrap.

6. Keeping tension on the wraps with the left thumb, begin to ease the needle through the fabric and wraps.

BULLION KNOT / CONTINUED

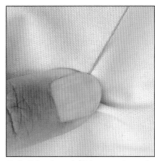

7. Continuing to keep tension on the wraps, pull the needle and thread through the wraps.

8. Pull the thread all the way through, tugging it away from you until a small pleat forms in the fabric. This helps to ensure a tight even knot.

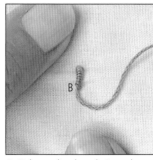

9. Release the thread. Smooth out the fabric and the knot will lie back towards B.

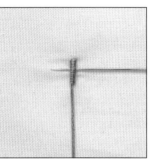

10. To ensure all the wraps are even, gently stroke and manipulate them with the needle while maintaining tension on the thread.

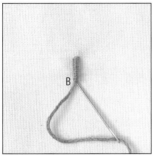

11. Take the needle to the back at B to anchor the knot.

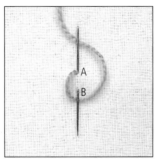

12. Pull the thread through and end off.

CHAIN STITCH

This very versatile stitch can be used as an outline or in close rows as a filling stitch. Take care not to pull the loops too tight as they will lose their rounded shape.

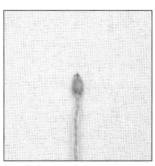

1. Bring the thread to the front at A. Take the needle from A to B, using the same hole in the fabric at A. Loop the thread under the tip of the needle.

2. Pull the thread through until the loop lies snugly around the emerging thread.

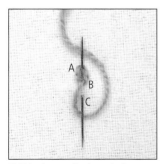

3. Take the needle through the same hole in the fabric at B and emerge at C. Ensure the thread is under the tip of the needle.

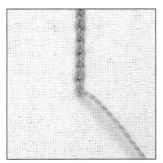

4. Pull the thread through as before. Continue working stitches in the same manner for the required distance.

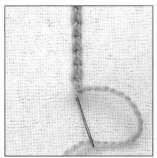

5. To finish, work the last stitch and take the needle to the back of the fabric just over the loop.

6. Pull the thread through to form a short straight stitch. End off the thread on the back of the fabric.

COUCHING

Couching can be used to work outlines or fill shapes. One or two foundation or laid threads are secured to the fabric with a second thread and tiny stitches.

These stitches hold the laid threads snugly, but do not squeeze them.

1. Bring the foundation thread to the front and lay it in the desired position on the fabric.

2. Bring the couching thread to the front just above the laid thread and near where it emerged from the fabric.

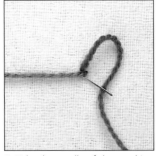

3. Take the needle of the couching thread over the laid thread and to the back of the fabric.

4. Pull the thread through to form the first couching stitch. Emerge a short distance away along the laid thread.

5. Take the couching thread over the laid thread and to the back of fabric as before.

6. Continue working stitches in the same manner to the end of the laid thread. Take both threads to the back of the fabric and end off.

DETACHED CHAIN

This stitch is commonly known as lazy daisy stitch. Other names are daisy stitch, knotted knot stitch, loop stitch, picot stitch, tied loop stitch, tail stitch and link powdering stitch.

Detached chain stitch is a looped stitch, which can be worked alone or in groups. It can also be used as a filling stitch with individual stitches placed at regular intervals over the space to be filled.

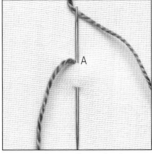

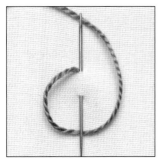

1. Bring the needle to the front at the base of the stitch at A. Take the needle to the back as close as possible to A. Emerge at the tip of the stitch.

2. Loop the thread in an anti-clockwise direction under the tip of the needle.

3. Keeping your left thumb over the loop, pull the thread through. The tighter you pull, the thinner the stitch will become.

4. To anchor the stitch, take the thread to the back just over the loop.

FLY STITCH

Fly stitch is an open detached chain stitch with many possible variations.

It is worked in the shape of a 'V' or 'Y' depending on the length of the anchoring stitch.

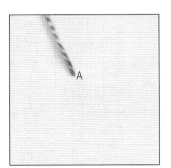 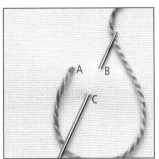 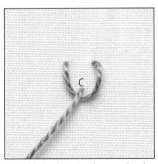 

1. Bring the thread to the front at A. This will be the left hand side of the stitch.

2. Take the needle to the back at B and emerge at C. Loop the thread under the tip of the needle and to the right.

3. Hold the loop in place under the left thumb. Pull the needle through until the looped thread lies snugly against C.

4. Take the thread to the back at the required distance below C to anchor the fly stitch.

FRENCH KNOT

The traditional French knot was worked with only one wrap, however today it is often worked with more.

A larger knot will look neater worked with more strands of thread rather than too many wraps.

1. Bring the thread to the front.

2. Hold the thread firmly with your left thumb and index finger 3cm (1 1/4") away from the fabric.

3. With your left hand, bring the thread over the needle. Ensure the needle points away from the fabric.

4. Wrap thread around the needle. Keeping the thread taut, begin to turn the point of the needle towards the fabric.

   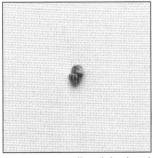

5. Take the needle to the back approx. 1 - 2 fabric threads away from the emerging thread.

6. Slide the knot down the needle onto the fabric. Pull the thread until the knot is firmly around the needle.

7. Slowly push the needle to the back of the fabric while holding the knot in place under your thumb. Begin to pull the thread through.

8. Continue to pull until the thread disappears under your thumb and is completely pulled through.

GHIORDES KNOT

Ghiordes knots are also known as Turkey work and single knot tufting. The velvety pile is formed by leaving every second stitch as a loop which is later cut and combed. Rows of knots are worked from left to right either away from you or towards you.

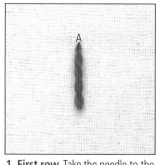

1. First row. Take the needle to the back at A on the left hand side. Pull the thread through, leaving a tail on the front of the fabric.

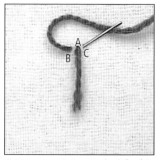

2. Emerge at B, just to the left of A. Take the needle to the back at C, just to the right of A.

3. Hold the tail taut and pull the thread through. Re-emerge at A just below the previous stitch.

4. Pull the thread through. With the thread below the needle, take the needle to the back at D.

5. Pull the thread through leaving a loop the same length as the tail. Bring the needle to the front at C and pull through. Take the needle to the back at E.

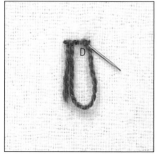

6. Pull the thread through. Bring the needle to the front at D, just below the previous stitch.

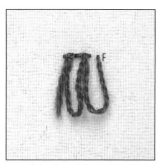

7. Pull the thread through. With the thread below the needle, take it to the back at F, leaving a loop on the front.

8. Continue to the end of the row. Ensure the last stitch is not a loop. Finish with the thread on the front. Trim, leaving a tail the same length as the loops.

9. Second row. Take the needle to the back of the fabric, directly above A. Pull the thread through, leaving a tail on the front.

10. Work the second row in the same manner as the first row.

11. Continue working the required number of rows in the same manner. Stand the loops up and trim them evenly. Do not trim them too short.

12. Alternate between combing and trimming until the stitches are the desired height and appearance.

LATTICE COUCHING

Lattice couching is one of the many variations of couched fillings. The design area is covered with a foundation of evenly spaced laid threads. The spacing of the diagonal stitches is determined by the thickness of the thread used. Where two laid threads cross, they are secured to the background with a small straight stitch. Lattice couching can be worked directly onto the fabric or over a satin-stitched shape.

1. Foundation. Bring the thread to the front near the left side of the shape at the upper edge, A.

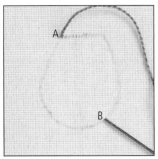

2. Take the needle to the back at B, on the lower right side of the shape.

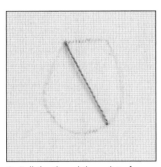

3. Pull the thread through to form a diagonal stitch.

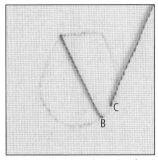

4. Bring the thread to the front at C, above B.

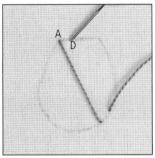

5. Take the needle to the back at D, to the right of A.

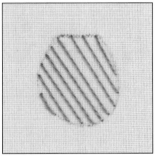

6. Pull the thread through. Continue working evenly spaced parallel stitches in the same manner until the entire area is covered.

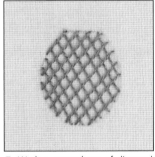

7. Work a second set of diagonal stitches over the design area in the opposite direction to form a pattern of diamonds.

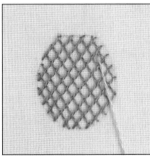

8. Couching. Using a new thread, bring it to the front directly below the first intersection on the upper right of the shape.

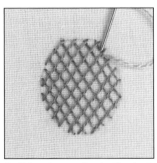

9. Take the needle to the back directly above the intersection. Pull through to complete the first couching stitch.

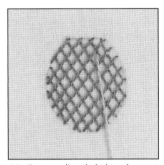

10. Emerge directly below the next intersection to the left.

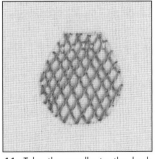

11. Take the needle to the back directly above the intersection and continue across the row in the same manner.

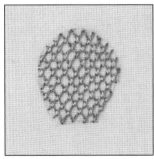

12. Repeat for the remaining intersections. Take the thread to the back and end off.

SATIN STITCH

Satin stitch is also known as damask stitch. Work with the fabric in a hoop and angle the needle under the outline when coming to the front or going to the back. Split stitch is used to outline the shape and gives a smooth, stable edge. When working a curve, fan the stitches on the outer edge and keep them close together on the inner edge.

1. Straight shape. Outline the shape to be filled with split stitch. This helps to create a neat edge.

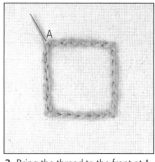

2. Bring the thread to the front at A, just outside the outline.

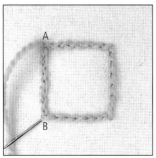

3. Take the needle to the back at B, just over the outline and directly opposite A.

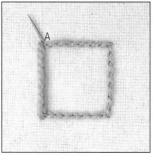

4. Pull the thread through. Emerge next to A, angling the needle from under the outline.

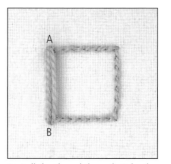

5. Pull the thread through. Take the needle to the back of the fabric next to B and pull the thread through.

6. Continue working stitches in the same manner until reaching the end of the shape. End off the thread on the back of the fabric.

7. Curved shape. When working a curved or complex shape, begin near the centre. Bring the thread to the front at A.

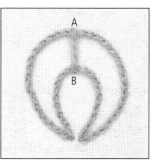

8. Take the needle to the back at B, directly below A. The stitch is at right angles to the shape at this point. Pull the thread through.

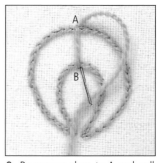

9. Re-emerge close to A and pull the thread through. Take the needle to the back near B, leaving a slightly narrower space between the stitches.

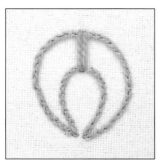

10. Pull the thread through to complete the second stitch.

11. Continue working stitches in the same manner, keeping each one at right angles to the outline. When one half is filled, end off the thread on the back.

12. Bring the thread to the front close to A. Fill the remaining half of the shape in the same manner.

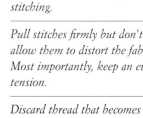

HINTS

When stitching with more than one strand of thread, 'strip' the thread before use (ie separate the strands and then put them back together).

Keep re-stripping the thread as you work to ensure the fullest stitch coverage. To do this, slide the needle down the thread onto the fabric. Separate the strands, then take the needle back up the thread to resume stitching.

Pull stitches firmly but don't allow them to distort the fabric. Most importantly, keep an even tension.

Discard thread that becomes worn and start with a new piece. Worn thread loses its sheen.

Work in a hoop and stab the needle up and down rather than skim it from one stitch to the next.

SOFT SHADING

Also known as thread painting, soft shading is a form of long and short stitch. Being a freer variation of this traditional stitch, the stitches are laid down with less uniformity and so it is possible to create a realistic blending of colour.

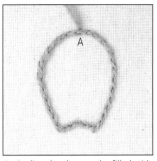

1. Outline the shape to be filled with split stitch. This helps to create a neat, well defined edge. Bring the thread to the front at A, just outside the outline.

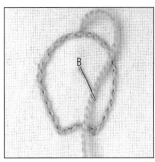

2. Take the needle to the back at B, within the shape.

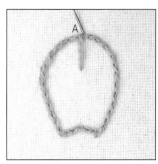

3. Pull the thread through. Emerge just beyond the outline very close to A.

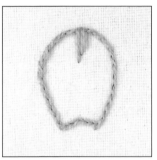

4. Pull the thread through. Work a second stitch which is slightly shorter than the first stitch.

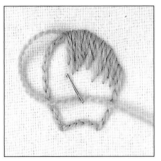

5. Continue working stitches very close together, fanning them to fit the shape. Alternate between long stitches and shorter stitches.

6. When the section is complete, take the thread to the back of the fabric and end off.

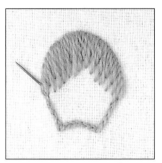

7. Using a darker shade of thread, bring the needle to the front, splitting a stitch of the previous row.

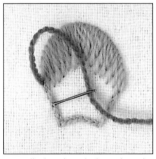

8. Pull the thread through. Take the needle to the back in the unembroidered area.

9. Work long and short stitches in the same direction as the first row, always emerging through a previous stitch. When complete, end off as before.

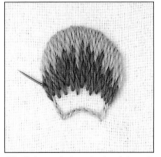

10. Using a darker shade of thread, bring the needle to the front, splitting a stitch of the previous row.

11. Repeat steps 8 and 9. When complete, end off as before.

SPLIT STITCH

Also known as Kensington outline stitch, split stitch can be used as an outline or as a filling stitch. It lends itself to subtle shading when it is worked in multiple rows to fill a shape.

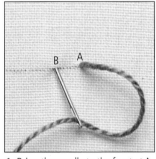

1. Bring the needle to the front at A. Take the needle to the back at B approximately 3mm (1/8") away.

2. Pull the thread through. Emerge at C in the centre of the first stitch, splitting the thread with the needle.

3. Pull the thread through to complete the first stitch and begin the second stitch.

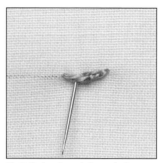

4. Take the needle to the back approximately 3mm (¹/₈") away.

5. Pull the thread through. Emerge through the centre of the second stitch.

6. Pull the thread through. Continue working stitches in the same manner.

STEM STITCH

Also known as crewel stitch, stem stitch is similar in appearance to outline stitch.

The thread is always kept below the needle, whereas in outline stitch it is kept above.

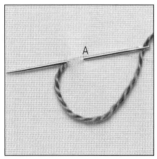

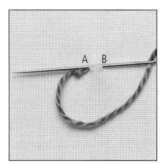

1. Bring the needle to the front at the left hand side of the line. With the thread below the needle, take it to the back at A. Re-emerge at the end of the line.

2. Pull the thread through. Again with the thread below the needle, take the needle from B to A.

3. Pull the thread through. Continue working the stitches in the same manner, always keeping the thread below the needle and the stitches the same size.

4. To end off, take the needle to the back for the last stitch but do not re-emerge. Secure the thread on the back with tiny back stitches.

STRAIGHT STITCH

Also known as stroke stitch, straight stitch is the most basic embroidery stitch.

It can be stitched in any direction and to any length and it forms the basis of many other stitches.

1. Bring the thread to the front at the beginning of the stitch, A.

2. Take the needle to the back at the end of the stitch, B.

3. Pull the thread through and end off on the back of the fabric.

4. Straight stitches worked at different angles.

STITCH DIRECTION
DIAGRAM

straight grain

CLASS OF 99 | *page 8*

STITCH DIRECTION DIAGRAM

straight grain

SPLASH | *page 9*

STITCH DIRECTION
DIAGRAM

straight grain

HALT! WHO GOES THERE | *page 10*

STITCH DIRECTION
DIAGRAM

straight grain

SUNDAY BEST | *page 11*

STITCH DIRECTION
DIAGRAM

straight grain

BOOK WORM | *page 12*

STITCH DIRECTION
DIAGRAM

straight grain

SHIP AHOY | *page 13*

STITCH DIRECTION
DIAGRAM

straight grain

BATHING BEAUTY | *page 14*

STITCH DIRECTION
DIAGRAM

straight grain

CLOWNING AROUND | *page 15*

STITCH DIRECTION
DIAGRAM

straight grain

DANCING QUEEN | *page 16*

STITCH DIRECTION
DIAGRAM

straight grain

HELLO HELLO HELLO | *page 17*

STITCH DIRECTION
DIAGRAM

straight grain

FLORENCE | *page 18*

STITCH DIRECTION
DIAGRAM

straight grain

SQUIRE | *page 17*